The Magic Is Inside You
Powerful & Positive Thinking For Confident Kids

Story By Cathy Domoney

Illustrations by Karen Davis

Previously Published As "Madeleine, Maddy & Midge"

D1361850

"I can see this book on every primary education establishment's shelf. It's such a great story and one that children will be able to understand and relate to. The characters are all believable and the language accessible. Your points at the end are all really helpful discussion tools and imaginative ideas. I would say the publishers, schools, psychologists, and parents are all going to love it! You are on to a winner here."
—Marie Fitzgerald, BEd (Hons)

"All children deserve to feel good about themselves, and this book helps them feel just that. The story appeals to children of all ages and will become a much-thumbed favourite. Parents and teachers will find it a useful aid for raising self-esteem through assemblies, circle times and bedtimes. What a way to boost their confidence!"
—Jess Caunter, primary Principal, BEd (Hons), NPQH

"You put something which is quite complex into simple terms that children can easily understand and relate to. I think all children would find comfort in your book, and I believe any child would find it empowering. I believe that you have something really special and valuable to say. Where was your book when I was growing up?!"
—Kerrie Clarke, Professional Artist and Mother

"This book offers children a clear and accessible story through which greater confidence and self-esteem can develop, and the suggestions and activities offered at the end of the story will be welcomed and used by many adults who support children in a broad range of settings."
—Sarah Hebe, Art Psychotherapist

ISBN-13 978-1985557253
ISBN-10 1985557258

For Ian, Skye, Tristan, Noah, Caleb & Théa Rose. x
-Cathy -

For G, T & J x
-Karen-

Madeleine was six years old. She was a sunshiny girl. She was smiley, giggly, and bouncy, and she was loved by many people .

"I love you, Madeleine," her daddy called.

"You always try your best. Well done, Madeleine," said Miss Poppet, her teacher.

"You are so scrumptious. We love you so much," whispered her mummy.

These words of love made the light inside of Madeleine shine brightly, brighter than the stars twinkling in the sky. They made her feel like she was floating in a rainbow bubble, high into the sun-filled air. They made her feel very happy, like she could fly to the moon in a rocket ship.

Yes, Madeleine was a very happy little girl—most of the time.

Madeleine had a secret friend called Maddy. Maddy's voice was exactly like Madeleine's but just a little bit smaller. Maddy was a wonderful friend to have, because she told Madeleine fantastic things. When Madeleine listened to Maddy, she felt very good about herself.

Maddy said, "Madeleine, you always try your best. You are so brave!" And Madeleine did feel brave.

"Madeleine, you are getting better and better at reading every day. Keep practicing. Well done!" And Madeleine did get better and better at reading.

"Madeleine you are so good at trying with your sums. Look how many you got right! Well done. You are learning so quickly!" And Madeleine did get better at her sums.

"Madeleine, so many people want to be your friend because you are so clever, kind, and funny." And more people did want to play with Madeleine, because she smiled more, laughed more, the light inside of her shone brightly, and she was fun to be around.

Madeleine liked listening to Maddy. It made her feel ...

Brave. Happy. Fantastic.

Sparkly. Shiny. Special.

As tall as a tree.

Clever. Amazing. Talented.

Colourful. Important. Bright.

Like a beautiful firework bursting in the night sky.

Smiley. Wonderful. Strong.

Unique. Loved. Safe.

As spectacular as a butterfly.

Madeleine liked listening to Maddy. It made her feel like she could do anything and the light inside her would shine as brightly as the sun.

Madeleine also had a secret friend called Midge. Midge's voice was exactly like Madeleine's but just a little bit smaller. Midge was not a very good friend to have at all. Midge told Madeleine horrible lies! When Madeleine listened to Midge, she worried and did not feel good about herself.

Midge told Madeleine, "This book is too hard. You can't read it! You're not as good at sums as you thought!" And Madeleine became less confident at reading and doing her sums.

"You're stupid and ugly. Nobody wants to be your friend!" And fewer children wanted to play with Madeleine, because she didn't smile or laugh very much, and the light inside of her was growing dim. She wasn't as much fun to be around, and she felt as though she was standing under a big, grey sky. She felt as if her tummy was crawling with bugs of all shapes and sizes, wriggling around inside her, making her ...

As sad and heavy as a rain cloud.

Grey. Grumpy. Frightened.
As quiet as a mouse.
Invisible. Tearful. Nervous.

As lost as a feather on a stormy wind.
Ugly. Flat. Lonely. Afraid.
As scared as a tortoise, hiding in his shell.
As tiny as an ant.
Like a sad, saggy balloon that has
lost all of its air.

Madeleine did not like listening to Midge. Midge made Madeleine feel useless and upset.

Madeleine felt very tired, and Midge started to talk to her more than usual. Midge talked and talked and just wouldn't stop. All of the sad and horrible things that Midge said started to fill Madeleine's head. This made Madeleine feel dizzy and ill.

Madeleine listened and believed all of the nasty things that Midge said. "You're not good enough, Madeleine! You really are a joke. You are rubbish. Nobody likes you!"

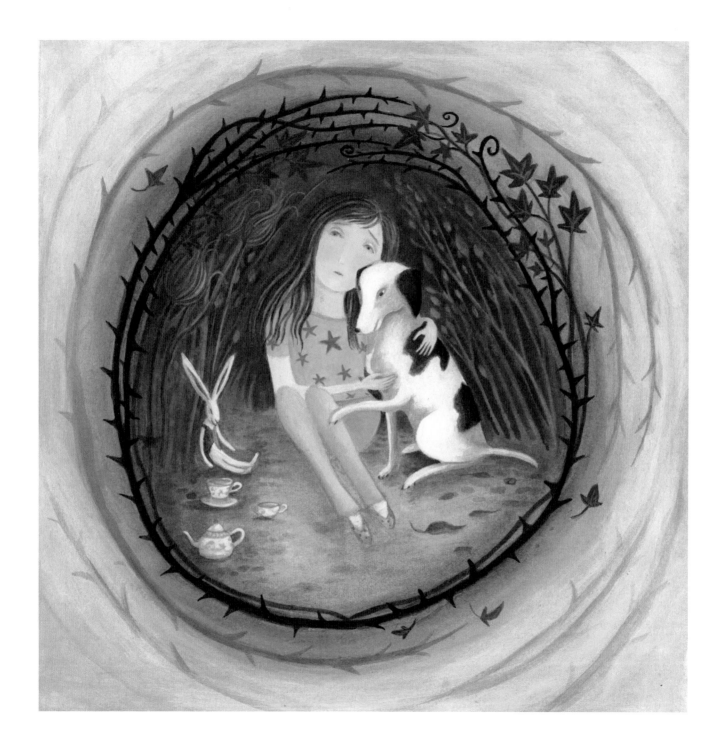

Madeleine had trouble sleeping, and she could not think clearly.

She snapped at the people around her.

She cried for no reason.

Soon Madeleine could not hear Maddy's voice clearly at all.

One day, Madeleine felt so upset and lost that she climbed up into her mummy's lap. Madeleine told Mummy how unhappy and scared she felt.

"Mummy, I wish I knew a magic spell to get rid of Midge, so that I could only listen to Maddy's kind words. I am worried that the light inside of me has gone out!" She buried her head into her mummy, and she cried and cried.

"Sweetheart, you need to listen to me now, because I have a very important secret to tell you," said Mummy.

"I know the magic to make Midge go away!"

Madeleine gasped. What could the secret be?

Madeleine leaned in close and listened carefully to what Mummy had to say.

"The magic is inside you, Madeleine!"

Madeleine felt confused, but then Mummy told her something truly amazing.

"The magic is that all you have to do is stop listening to Midge's lies. This will take away her power, and she will start to disappear. Soon she will be gone, and the light inside of you will shine like the brightest of stars."

Right then and there, from that moment onwards, Madeleine made up her mind to only listen to Maddy, no matter how hard Midge tried to be heard.

Madeleine chose to believe all of the wonderful things that Maddy said and decided to be ...

Happy!

Now and then, Midge tried telling Madeleine more lies. Shush, Midge, that's enough, said Madeleine. I can do it! You can't tell me how to feel anymore.
You're rubbish, not me!
And just like a bursting bubble ...
Midge went POP!

Her voice disappeared, and ...

"Well done, Madeleine!" Maddy sang out. "You are so wonderful and brave! You're a superstar! You can do anything! You should be so proud of yourself!"

Madeleine beamed with delight, ran over to Mummy, and hugged her tight. Then, with a skip and a smile, she ran outside into the garden to play—happy, giggling, and strong.

From that day onwards, there were still times when Midge would try to re-appear and make Madeleine feel bad. But Madeleine was clever. She remembered that she had the magic power inside of her to choose, and she would listen to Maddy and tell Midge to "Shush!"

Madeleine's days were then filled with laughter, happiness, and love, and the light inside of her shone beautiful and bright once more.

For Parents, Carers and Teachers

I have included the activities below to guide you in using this book as a tool to help further develop children's self-esteem.

Points to share with children

- Ask your child if they have little characters like Maddy & Midge. Explore what sort of messages they have in their inner dialogue. This can be really revealing and help you to understand where your child is coming from and what, if anything, they are struggling with. You could ask them to draw themselves in the middle of the paper, then draw their 'alter egos' to the left and the right of them and write (or have you scribe) the thoughts that they provide.
- How did Madeleine feel when she listened to Maddy? (Happy, Strong, Brave.) How do you know? (Adjectives and colours used.) Recap "Happy feelings" page.
- Have you ever had these feelings? When? Why? (List them together and discuss.)
- What did Madeleine feel like when she listened to Midge? How do you know? (Sad adjectives and dull colours used.) Recap "Sad feelings" page.

- Have you ever felt like you had worried creepy-crawlies in your tummy? What made you feel this way? What kind of thoughts were in your head? How could you help yourself to feel better? (Stop the bad thoughts and turn them in to good ones. For example, "I am bad at math" becomes "I listen carefully in my math lessons, and every day I am getting better and better!" This can also be reinforced verbally by you as the trusted adult, to keep giving the child positive messages about the things they have anxiety over.) For example: "Wow, you are getting better and braver with your learning every day! That is so brilliant! Good job!"

- Have you ever felt like a beautiful, bright firework shining brightly in the night sky? What made you feel this way? What sort of thoughts were in your head? (List in poster format and discuss. This is an excellent resource to have if ever the children are feeling low again. Revisiting it during low moments reminds them of their strengths, how they can feel positive, and reminds them of how to get there again.)

- What happened when Madeleine decided to stop listening to Midge? (She was happy! The colour returned to her life, and she could listen to Maddy again.)

- How did Madeleine feel when Midge went "pop"? (Relieved. Discuss why. Because listening to Midge drained Madeleine and made her too scared to try. Listening to the positive messages from Maddy made her feel as though she could do anything.)

- What will Madeleine need to do if Midge tries to come back? (Choose to change her thoughts and listen to Maddy instead. Tell Midge to shush!)

- Where was the magic to break Midge's spell? (Madeleine had the power to focus on the positive all along.)
- For older readers: Why did Maddy and Midge look and sound so much like Madeleine? Because they are Madeleine; they represent her positive and negative thoughts.

Suggested Activities

- Locker/Drawer/Pillow Post: Write your children a secret letter to be placed under their pillow, or in their school drawer/locker. Tell them all the things that they are doing right. Let them know how proud you are of them and all of the amazing wonderful things that you admire and love about them. I have done this with great effect. Sometimes, a small, simple surprise such as this can have a significant and long-lasting positive impact.
- Who are your secret friends? You can encourage your children to draw a picture of themselves and their little characters. They can name them, be playful with them. This will help them to separate their thoughts into what is useful and what is harmful. The children must understand that they have the choice of who they listen to; the children always have the power. The characters are not to be used as scapegoats for bad choices!

- Dream Diary: Using words and pictures, write or draw in a special scrapbook all of the fantastic wonderful things about your children and also all of the things that they would like to achieve. This is a terrific focus for your children and a very positive way to help them to remain focussed on goals (which can easily be changed) and believe in themselves.

- Celebration Poster: A lovely activity for great self-esteem is to make a poster with your child's name as the centre, and then friends and family everyone can add all of the fabulous wonderful skills, talents, and attributes belonging to that child, all around their name. This provokes a feeling of uniqueness and of being special and important. I have used this with individual children, within the family and within the classroom setting. It is a wonderful experience for all involved, and the focus child often does not realise the good things that others feel about them. This raises their self-esteem and helps them to further achieve and live up to the opinions of others. Get creative! Use glitter, pictures out of cut-up magazines, stickers, colour, etc. The brighter the better! It is great to have as a resource if the child slips back into negativity, as it boosts them quickly back up again.

- Catch them being good at school: If you are working with a child who has very low self-esteem which has manifested itself in a deterioration of their behaviour, it is very important to focus on every single thing that they get right. For example, one boy who I inherited in my new class when I used to teach had reached the point of being excluded from school. One bad choice followed another relentlessly. He had been labelled as a troublemaker, and he lived up to his hype! We started his self-esteem journey by creating a sticker-chart for every playtime he had for the whole week, every week. Every playtime, he was awarded a sticker for having chosen to play nicely with someone new (as he had no friends). He was also rewarded for having made it through the playtime without having physically hurt anyone in any way. We decided upon how many stickers would be his realistic target to achieve. If he met his weekly target, a celebration poster was sent home to his very supportive single parent at the end of the week. It was astounding how quickly this child made progress. Why? Because as the adults in his life, we cared, we wanted him to succeed, we believed he could do it, and we made sure that he could achieve and celebrate it. Every kindness, every polite word, every good choice, no matter how small, was celebrated. He lived up to the expectations and the praise, and his behaviour and his academic progress began to improve. Parents could share this approach with teachers and suggest that they try it.

- Catch them being good at home: These collected stickers could become a voucher to cash in for money, a trip to the park, chocolate, a cinema trip—whatever your budget and your agreement with the child. An important note about the giving of stickers is that once given, they should never be taken away as a punishment. If a bad choice is made, think of another consequence like an early bedtime, no TV, etc. Never take away what the child has worked so hard to earn, otherwise this undermines the whole process, and the child is likely to give up. Also, whatever the voucher represents must be realistic, as it must be delivered to the child upon completion as the reward.

- Flip It!: Sit with your child and scribe for them all of the things that they are worried or unhappy about, and turn them into statements. Then one by one, flip those statements from negative to positive. For example, "People do not like me" becomes "I am strong inside. I am a clever, funny person who makes good choices, and people want to be my friend." Often these changes in our thought process affect the way that we act around others, the way we think about ourselves; our general behaviour changes for the better. Therefore, our expectations and the expectations of those around us change for the positive. These affirmations, when used regularly, are simple and yet can be very effective. The affirmations will evolve as the child achieves and grows; their aspirations will change. Hopefully these aspirations will become greater and more ambitious. These can be read aloud and shared every morning over breakfast or every evening before bed or both!

- Separate the behaviour from the child: If your child has been having difficulty with their choices and behaviour, it is important for them to face the consequences and accept responsibility for what they have done. (Please note, some adults have difficulty achieving this!) However, it is very important that it is their behaviour that is labelled and not their character. If your behaviour is labelled as bullying, for example, behaviour can be relatively easily changed through guidance on how to make good choices. If the child is labelled a bully, that makes it harder to shake off. It gives people the impression that that it is who they are, rather than a reflection of bad decisions they made once. Once this has been done, they must be allowed to move on and leave it behind. This means that the behaviour or incident is not to be referred to as a reminder by anyone. The new and improved choices and behaviour are referred to and reinforced as much as possible. For example, if there is a "slip" in behaviour, the positive lists and posters can be used. You could explain to the child what went wrong and why. Then you can say thank goodness that they normally make such fantastic choices and have so many wonderful qualities. Refer to the posters and remind the child that they are fabulous and can make good choices.

- As the adult, it is your role to be clear about what is expected from the child, as well as the rewards and sanctions that have been agreed upon and put in place. The child needs to feel safe while they put the changes in place, so they need to be clear and consistent about what they need to do. They need a supportive environment in which to learn about positive and negative consequences. Implementing safe and fair sanctions is an expression of love. You are helping the child understand about reasonable behaviours, accountability, and consequences. These are lessons they will need to function in the "outside world."

Dear Friends,

I hope you and your children have enjoyed this story. The most important thing to remember is that every child is different and that there is no "right" or "wrong" way to help them! As long as we begin from a position of love, patience, and respect, we are on the right track. This book has offered you some suggestions for strategies that I have used with various children over the years that have proven successful. You may find that these examples may not exactly fit your child. My hope is that it will be a starting point for you to generate your own ideas for the unique child in your care. I hope that it has opened up a line of communication for you to further develop and explore with your child or children.

One thing I do know is that if you are reading this book, then we share something fantastic in common: our love for children. You have picked up my book for a reason. You want to help the child or children in your care. This is a wonderful and loving act, and I applaud you. We care about them, respect them, and our ambition is to help them be the best that they can be, whatever that means to them personally. We want to help them to recognize their uniqueness and to reach their magnificent potential.

I wish you love, luck, and success on your journey, and I celebrate the fact that your child's self-esteem is very important to you. It fills me with hope that our future generations can be more confident, self-aware, empowered human beings capable of making real future change for the better.

May you and your child shine as brightly as a firework in the night sky.

Light and love,

-Cathy-

About the Author

Cathy Domoney works as a coach and inspirational speaker, focussing on self-esteem and confidence work with clients both young and old, as well as holding teaching seminars on living with the law of attraction, successful parenting and theories of modern-day philosophers. Cathy is a qualified primary teacher of eighteen years and is passionate about self-esteem and confidence work with adults and children alike. She holds Diplomas in Hypnotherapy and Counselling, and also holds a Bachelor's Degree in Sociology and has extensively studied Life Coaching. Cathy discovered early on in her teaching career how vital a pupil's view of themselves and their capabilities was to their academic attainment, behaviour, and happiness. When teaching full time, she held the position of personal, health, social, and moral education coordinator. This allowed her to work directly with pupils and colleagues on self-esteem issues, and she saw how positive thinking could powerfully impact a child's experience in the world. Cathy's mission is to raise the confidence of as many children as she can through her stories and help them to achieve the individual greatness that each child has inside of them. She hopes that this can contribute to a much happier, more well-rounded future generation. Cathy was born and raised in Wiltshire, England. She now resides happily in Adelaide, South Australia, with her husband, Ian, and their five wonderful children.

To contact Cathy for interviews or to secure her services, please see details below:

cathydomoney@gmail.com

www.cathydomoney.com

Facebook @cathydomoneybliss
Facebook @cathydomoneyconfidentkids
Twitter @domchick
LinkedIn Cathy Domoney
Instagram Cathy Domoney

Acknowledgements

Many thanks to my editor Jennifer Douglas @ Good Gabble Review and to Sabine Verhack @ Sabine Verhack Photography for all of your help and guidance with the formatting of this book.

Thank you to my daughter Skye for helping me with the technology x

Thanks to my husband, Ian, for his unwavering support. x

Many thanks to my fabulous and dedicated launch team; details of the whole crew can be found on my website www.cathydomoney.com

Thank you to all of my SPS Community for helping me and supporting me throughout this publishing journey.

Made in the USA
Middletown, DE
18 August 2020